Sri Lankan

Theology

A Short Introduction

R T B ABEYSINGHE

Also by the author

*Ecclesiastes, Ecclesia and Existentialism: Some Experiential Permutations on the Essence of Being.

* The Last XV: Reflections on the Concept of the 'Religious Utopia' in the Private School Tradition in Sri Lanka.

* A Theology of Anxiety: Biblical Stories on How God makes Sense out of Worry.

* The Local Foreigners: Legacy of Socialization of the Ecclesia Anglicana

*Christian Worship and Liturgy: History and Modernity.

*The Architect: Basil Jackson and the future of Theological Education in Sri Lanka.

*Anxiety in Existential Psychotherapy and in Buddhist Counselling: A Comparative Conceptual Study.

*Tentmaker Ministry Revisited.

* Chaplaincy in a Multi Faith Context.

* Church Administration: A Simple Guide to the Task of Church Management in the Sri Lankan Context

* Myth, Misery and Mystery: Principles, Practice and Problems of Holistic Education

Sri Lankan Theology

A Short Introduction

2020

R T B ABEYSINGHE

R T B Abeysinghe

rtbabeysinghe@gmail.com

Printed by Creative Printers

DEDICATION

To all who tired for a local theology

CONTENTS

Preface

Foreword

PREFACE

In 2020 I was assigned to teach a course 'Introduction to Indian Christian Theology'. This course challenged me in several ways. In our 57th year at the Theological College of Lanka we have not been able to have a course on Introduction to Sri Lankan Theology. Currently we embed it when we teach the Indian Theology course.

The question also rose whether we have anything substantial to offer in terms of a theology from a Sri Lankan perspective. Further on, whether we are at all interested in documenting the thoughts of many who have gone before us. It is unlikely that 70 years will pass in a country known for its strict education for theological thinkers not to contribute substantial.

With motivation but also with much humility I set on the task of promulgating a series of reflections. With motivation as it was a great privilege to write something along these lines, eventhough imperfect it can be and humility as I may certainly not be the most scholarly to write something on this subject.

In the same manner I have also found three unique features of this book which assisted me in being motivated and being humble. The first of course is that this is a short introduction. It does not say that it ventures any deeper than the surface but captures several elements in a simple interpretation.

The second is that this book is more about the present rather than the theologians of the old, this is more in line with the challenges, thinkers and the way forward in a Sri Lankan Theology.

Finally, it keeps many options open both in theory and practice for meaningful dialogue to take place in the future. It does not say that this is complete even if it is a short introduction and hopefully opens the discussion.

In an independent country for nearly seventy we have engaged in this task and it must be our hope that what we have done is cherished and recorded so that our drop of contribution becomes of value to the sea of theological reflection.

I thank God, my family and colleagues, many friends and readers who have helped me in this process. It is also my privilege to thank Rev Leslie Dareeju who graciously undertook the task of writing the foreword to this book. His introduction to this work, and his own work and contribution towards a local theology are well appreciated.

R T B Abeysinghe
Feast of Ss Simon and Jude, 2020

FOREWORD

You are holding a book which will be a steppingstone to many books in the days to come in relation to the Sri Lankan Christian theology. It has been my pleasure to know Fr. Rasika Abeysinghe since 2010 in a friendship that has gone from mere acquaintance to partnership in the theological education and formation ministry. Fr. Rasika critically analyses various factors of the Sri Lankan Christian identity in relation to culture, traditions, and the multifaith society of Sri Lanka. Examples of contextual theology, drawing from our rich history, culture, religiosity etc are well documented. However, as an academic field in theology, we are at a relatively younger stage when compared to other countries. Unlike other academic disciplines in secular universities the study, research, publication, and wider communication of same is yet to be established.

It is encouraging to see that as we are now completing seventy years of independence, that promising features of developing perspectives of theology from a Sri Lankan point of view, is taking place. We live in the shadow, as it were, of periods of Church History that have produced many men and women of deepest piety who have witnessed widespread and lasting Christian theology of Sri Lanka. We thank both the Mainline Church and the many partners who have assisted us and who have motivated us towards this purpose. Sri Lankan Christian theology has much to offer to the world Christian community and also to the academia and it is our hope that this will become reality in the years to come.

I read the book over the week and then embarked several themes that are worth pondering upon as we reflect on how we live our faith in and through culture. The book brings a more recent look at theologizing within the faculty and a bibliographical resource that will promote further work and study.

Through the task is great it is our pleasure to introduce this book to anyone who is interested in getting an overview of the topic. It is certainly hoped that we will see further such works as we continue to promote and develop academia on a unique Sri Lankan theology.

Rev Leslie Dareeju

November 2020

1. WHY A SRI LANKAN THEOLOGY?

All theology comes into life based on its context. In the modern times we find many terms that comes in front of the word theology. When considering countries, Asian and Latin American and African theologies have for long become part and parcel in theological circles. Contexts can also be personalized such a Black, Hispanic, Feminist etc theology.

There is debate as to whether theology can be born without a context. Hence, the struggle of the traditional theorists of systematic theology and the newer contextual theology. The issue of relegating theology from a context as merely a contextual theology comes with it the added disadvantage that that these theologies might not contribute to an already existing and 'accredited' line of thinking in faculties.

These become realized as each context has something more to add. Each context offers a unique contribution. Even in the case it does not offer something unique it's

the context itself becomes a hopeful seedbed where new interpretations can come to life. Theology in
the Asian and African contexts have become thrown into the spotlight making these, centres where contextual imagining has come into light in the modern day.

The shift of the first, second and third millenniums of Christianity in the African, European and Asian contexts is becoming a reality. In this sense each of the Asian countries have become contributors towards this common cause. India, Japan, Philippines, Korea the list will grow in the years to come. In that regard Sri Lanka must also contemplate what it has to offer to this ongoing discussion.

Sri Lanka, itself has a Christian genesis of at least quarter ofa millennium, leaving alone the period of the Nestorians. The culture, ethic and doctrinology has had more than enough time to integrate with the local culture, ethic and common doctrinology. Sri Lankan Christianity had also achieved a relative independence from foreign rule for almost seven decades. While one may question that in the global place, full freedom is never achieved this is also a substantial time for effective dialogue to have taken place.

We would like to furnish below a few of these possible contributions that have unconsciously taken place. The first must be multi religiosity. This is of course true to all eastern countries as they have more of a lived through religiosity rather than the west which was 'introduced' into other faiths. In the same time Sri Lanka's uniqueness is that it houses all major religious traditions and the majority partner is Buddhism. The situation can be paralleled to Thailand and Burmawhere the major constituent is a non theistic faith. Faith seeking in a non faith atmosphere itself can be a daunting task. It also takes much creativity to inculcate one's faith within a sphere where much of what is described in faith terms become obsolete to a major portion of the public.

The second aspect will be the colonized faith perspective. All religious traditions in Sri Lanka are exported, prominent among these is Buddhism which grew in this country after the subsequent decline in India. Yet all of these faiths have found the courage to inculturateupto some deal in their day to day affairs and faith practice. This is true of the Christian faith as well. From being under colonial rule, whose faith also corresponded with the faith they wanted to nurture, the idea of western influence was heavy. Therefore its strains can never be extinguished.

Another important aspect in this discussion is the fact that Sri Lanka is a developing country. Earlier called as third world countries, these countries are working towards areas such as democracy, self sufficiency, rights, equality etc which much of the developed countries have achieved. That would also point to the fact that Sri Lanka has with it issues that might complicate situations in this manner. For an example eventhough the country is styled socialist democratic, many critics have questioned if either of these are present within the life of the country. To add to this poverty, unemployment, injustice, ethnic and religious conflict, gender violence etc also highlight in a never ending saga of issues that are not perfectly aligned with a developed country.

Finally,the country itself has a rich cultural and emotional underlining as opposed to western countries. This is a theme which we can develop as the book takes shape. It merely means that culture precedes the life ethic of citizens. Therefore culture plays a major role in religious, social and economical issues. Therefore it must also play a similarly important role in theologizing, The now famous 'gospel and culture' primarily became coined after the push of the Asian and African countries who valued culture asa blanket that covered thinking theological minds.

Then to follow up on the question that we try to discuss at the beginning of this chapter is, what a Sri Lankan theology? The answer is a Sri lankan theology is one which is contributory of all the above factors. The theologizing is placed in the context of Sri Lanka present, past and future. It takes into consideration the geography, history, demography, economy, sociology and many such factors that makes us who we are. And when we term the 'we' in this statement it also takes into consideration that this theologizing comes from many factors of the country and from a diversity of people. It is very hard to find the general Christian who theologizes in this context. The context makes the reasoning and the intent of reasoning.

In this regard when we talk of a theology borne out of Sri Lanka we emphasize that it's not one but many. And going forward we will look at the many examples why this becomes so. Unlike the western model. where we can think of faith in one direction with one goal, our context is diversified. It calls for us to think in the shoes of the many voices heard but also unheard. One reason why contextuality becomes messy in reasoning is also because we do it on multiple fronts. Let us then proceed with how we can accomplish this in reflection.

2. METHOD IN CONTEXTUAL THEOLOGY

In the discussion of a theology that is Sri Lankan we inevitably keep on talking of a contextual theology. While there maybe much more authoritative studies on this subject, some aspects of theologizing in context must be discussed especially with regard to method.

Methodology on theology has for a long time being anissue that was a 'given' in the sense that the process was not changeable. Thanks to the marginalized voices at a previous time frame, the methodology leading to faith understanding has changed. It is now possible to inculcate a different view which may sometime challenge systematic theological method and rationale. We will look at the use of method in the traditional four areas of resources of Bible, tradition, reason and experience.

When we look at the Biblical interpretation in method, we find that re-reading the word of God became the cornerstone of the new liberation oriented theologies in the Latin American countries. As our primary tool of visible knowledge the use of the Bible and its interpretation become paramount to the method in contextualization. In re-reading the Bible we are called to understand the truth that transpires, actually comes to anon western country. While the society and traditions of this society bypasses that of our own we are called to think in the same light as a country in Asia.

When we look at the stories of Jesus we need to input the Sri Lankan idiom and ethos into each passage, so that while not changing the narrative we change the outcome or goal of the intention. Jesus' message to the marginalized then becomes the message to the cornered in our society. The love that binds our faith becomes the one that must be realized in a multi faith context. The concepts of justice and peace of the prophets, become the issues we face today of corruption and politicization. And the historical journey of faith becomes the story of the Church and the story of the Church in the Bible gives hope to each community spread across this island in searching for unity.

Tradition is another aspect we have so far conserved with utmost loyalty. This is present when we are unable to relieve even from the ecclesiology of the western culture. And most times we do perform liturgies which the westerners might even disavow. The issue with tradition is also the problem with its meaning. Unless we follow something to the word then there is no tradition. It might as well be a question between tradition or no tradition. And when we as Christians believe in the legacy of a faith that was planted in the country it is difficult to relieve ourselves of the tentacles of Church traditions and its relations.

The understanding that we must be 'Ceylonese Christians' has taken a long time to be implanted in this country. Still we may find non Christians who may denounce Christianity a western construct. On this front the only solution for a change in method must be the generation of a local ideology in our faithpractice. This can be from how we worship and our liturgies, it must take into consideration our contribution to the national society, it must develop policy and practices which make even the local village church become part of the community. In terms of the arts and crafts we must be able to show forth the differences of a Sri Lankan touch in our faith practice.

The next component is probably the hardest of all these aspects. As it deals with our emotions, it deals with our anxieties and it deals with the way we look at things. Coming from an Asian culture which is conservative we have grown to reason in a different manner. With the advent of Christianity we look at our faith also in the reasoning that we find in western concepts. To give one example the notion of salvation which was imbibed into us is still what the foreign interpretations have given without any understanding of cultures and religions. We are called to reason with regard to our situation realizing that we have been taught might not be suitable for every occasion.

Finally and most importantly as we discuss of method in theology, we rely on experience. The experience that is ours in totality. It takes into consideration colonialism, war, unrest, discrimination, instability in governance, agricultural economy, religions, communities who have lost their voices, the voices of labourers farmers displaced and plantation workers, the issues of drugs and violence, the clash of cultures and classism, extremism and the many similar wordings with its own set of examples we have witnessed throughout our history. It is a journey where we say that we now need to practice and think of our faith in terms of who we are and we give priority to our experiences.

The discussion of the above is by no means exhaustive. A work can be built on each aspect over and over again. The main concern here is not only that we discuss these aspects but we try to inculcate it from our Sunday school to Theological education. The transformation is not an easy one, it calls for us to in a way denounce the Christianity from the west almost fully. While the west may not think of this as disrespectful we as Christians may have a much harder time in adapting this into our faith experience and journey. We must realize that every theology is contextual and that the Bible and Jesus' story are all part of contextuality. Yet we practice the same truths in different contexts and we need to uphold these with a spirit and understanding that makes sure that we are now catering the surrounding that we are presently living. Many Asian and African countries have made some progress in this transition yet not fully. The Sri Lankan version is still at an early stage yet we hope that our methodology might make sense to us as well as to outsiders in the years to come.

3. HISTORY OF THEOLOGICAL EDUCATION AND REFLECTION

For this purpose, we are concentrating primarily on the protestant churches in Sri Lanka and specifically the main line churches. The history of main line churches in Sri Lanka begins with the advent of the Dutch and the British. It makes it mark mainly in the mid 19th century where an explosion of denominations and missionaries are allowed to propagate their faith. We will look at the main resources and processes that made theologizing possible from the historical stand point.

Theological reflection and education was readily available to all Christians even from the start of the time of missionaries in that it was controlled. On the reflection front, freedom was available but apart from a personal view point there was no future for this thinking. In education other than catechism the education of clergy was mainly in foreign lands and its change was experienced in the mid of the 20th century with the

Theological college of lanka, Cathedral institute and the like.

Of courseSri Lankan Christians had the opportunity to reflect in terms of local songs, idiom, customs eventhough it was not encouraged. One main aspect that is related to this will be the prayer book translation and Bible translation. Both of these components can be deduced as components of theological reflection and education. It is so because in this task we are called to think of the Biblical truth in terms of where we are and who we are. It is of course doubtful that when we look at the literature before independence that effective theologizing took place. The mental bondage was upto some level greater than the physical when it comes to colonialism.

When we look at institutions there is ample evidence that places such as the Ecumenical Institute for Study and Dialogue, Satyodaya, Tulana, Devasaranaramaya were part of this ministry. The work of Ashrams was also part of this special mission as the local ecclesiology coupled with local thinking can be observed in these institutions. These were all accredited to persons who braved the storms and made it possible for an independent thinking. The making of the Theological college of Lanka is possibly the high point in this section. This is credited to as the first ecumenical and theological venture of all our mainline churches. The emphasis of building this college as a seminary, lay education centre and an interfaith collaborative centre was in line with training staff to become localized in their settings and to proclaim faith in culture.

The success if that may be the best word to use of the college might be critiqued but certainly the intention process has been laid. Currently all ministers who serve the mainline churches are products of the college and have spent time going through an indigenized syllabus that has been made with the Serampore college in India. The alliance with Serampore also with its critics, is upto a greater deal beneficial as this institute has achieved a gospel and culture trend through its mission. The path for our college to be on par with this would require further investment and commitment.

In terms of looking at other resources we look at the work of individuals who are deemed great in our history mainly for opening the way for a Sri Lanka theology. The work of D T Niles is of great importance as he developed an ecumenical yet a local framework for theology dispensation. In the same manner Bishop Lakdasa who was in the forefront of the indigenous movement with the example of the Diocese of Kurunagala was Bishop Lakshamn who was revolutionary in his work in justice and peace together with social movements are most worthy of mention.

The list is then continued with theologians such as Wesley Ariarajah and ShanthaPremawardhana who developed frameworks of interfaith collaboration. The same might also be recognized of Yohan Devananda and Lynn De Silva who pioneered work in Buddhism in study, dialogue and practice. Specific work must be mentioned of Donald Kanagaratnam, Jeffrey

Abeysekera, Duleep De Chikera and KumaraIllangasinghe who pioneered work in dialogue, reconciliation, nation building and liberation orientedtheology. The work of Rex Joseph in Biblical studies and literature will also be edged in memory while more recently work has been done on the Thamil missions and Christology by modern theologians. Albert Jebanesan developed much on communication while SarathWikremsinghe built on history of Christianity in Sri Lanka.

There is also many works that are archived in the Church History Documentation Centre at Pilimatalawa where historical evidence of theological reflection can be found. The work of the College journal, 'Sri Lanka Journal of Theological Reflection' is of paramount importance as this is for the moment the main piece of writing that connects our academia with the world. Many contributors have made their mark through this journal and have brought forward many details of the intricacies of Sri Lankan theologizing. There are also several books that have been published by individual authors who have worked on separate areas of interest. The liturgies of the Church and the experimental versions are also of great importance as these open up local theologizing. While many have remained experimental due its non recognition on a wider scale many challenging aspects of theology can be gauged from same.

The history of Sri Lankan theology is not complete without mention of the arts and the crafts. From hymns, to design from lyrics to dress from altar arrangement to dances and the many, these have been constant reminders that a local theology does exist. While some may downplay these as mere customs that have been adapted, we do realize that Sri Lanka is still young in terms of developing theology own theology. And when we go forth there will be more than can be traced from our faith practices that enhance our appreciation of a Sri Lankan theology.

4. TRINITARIAN THEOLOGY

God, the concept and the operation of God is the first step in theology. In a country which the majority of people profess a 'atheistic' or agnostic philosophy, it is challenging to even discuss the issue of a Supreme being. At most times the intention of doing so will be met with skepticism and ridicule. We will look at brief theological underpinnings as we work out the Trinity within this context.

In Buddhism there have been ample evidence to suggest of thinking about God. One of these is of course in relation to Mahayana Buddhism where allocation is made for theism. The second is the equation , like in Aloysius Peiris of the ultimate reality in terms of characteristics such as wisdom, light, finality, peace, enlightenment etc. Thirdly the development of agnosticism can be made to good use in that God becomes the creator but after creation the salvation of humanity does not remain dependent on the concept of God. This is also true of early Christian theologies. The issue in a Buddhist background with regard to God has been the presence of evil. Yet it is surprising that for a religion that places much emphasis on personal conduct and ethics, the link between human error and evil is not cemented well. While in theism the work of people does not guarantee liberation, and in the latter it does. This can be one of the main issues in understanding divinity in our context. However, why Buddhism is agnostic is also linked to the Lord Buddha who said that through testing everything can be ascertained. In that regard, the concept itself is not missing but with the subordination of theism in Buddhism to below humanity, the understanding of an Ultimate Reality can be surrounded in uncertainty.

The idea of salvation in the Sri Lankan context has once again been a dilemma. Once issue with regard to same can be the oriental understanding that leads to understand liberation in a full sense. Rather than the soul which is liberated, the emphasis on the totality of self and the world can be understood in this manner. Jesus as Saviour has brought varied interpretations into making salvation total. While there is more than enough evidence of Jesus' mission for a 'comprehensive' salvation this aspect can be furthered and linked to the 'work' aspect of Jesus rather than that of the faith aspect. The suffering and crucifixion of Jesus finds much focus even in Buddhists where the work of Jesus as sacrificial can be linked to many suffering that is present through which salvation is derived in the Buddhist understanding.

The work Lynn De Siva on 'Anatta' or no soul has opened up discussion between the two faiths where commonality is present for most time. As in Buddhism the understanding of the soul is absent and, even if a saviour concept can be promulgated, the work of the saviour becomes of difficult understanding. Yet this is an opportune time where much research and discussion can be done with regard to the comparisons that can be made between God the Son and the similar understanding in a primarily Buddhist context. However the personhood that brings reality in Jesus is of constant appeal in a context of ethics and suffering.

If the concept of God the Son has its difficult phase within the context, the concept of God the Spirit finds even more difficulty. The idea of a Holy Spirit becomes incompatible because of the inability of empirical data. As Buddhism operates mainly on the empirical working sphere the admission to a working that is not visible can be causal of this. Yet once again a direct relation can be brought with the spirit that makes people do things and the larger Spirit of God which speaks to humanity.

There can be also a link that can be made in the form of motivation and good fruits. The insistence that we are all motivated to do good and its relation with the eight fold path which starts with eight 'good' intentions can be worked out to develop a framework where eventhough unknowingly we are influenced by the Spirit. The good leading to good and the bad vice versa can be directed in this line of thinking as well. With the concept of transmigration and rebirth with the Christian understanding of life after life this can further be aligned with the work of the Spirit. And finally the main comparison of God the Spirit as truth can be of great importance to the ongoing discussion as the truth becomes vital in terms of a religion that dwells on wisdom and seeking wisdom. There can be progress made on these fronts once again as all parties in the discussion are privy to parts of their faith that can still be developed.

The Trinitarian God can be of a dilemma when discussed at an agnostic level. But with each aspect of the persons of the Trinity being of key concern even to the Buddhists who form the majority of the context, the relation can be made effectively. This is so as the aspect of creation, redemption and sanctification can be discussed quite openly and widely in this context. It opens gateways into the person as well as the world. In a philosophy where the person and the world alone is present the third aspect of God can be brought in as that community and which relates very much to salvation. There is the understanding of 'kaaya' where the work of Buddha is divided into three 'kaaya' which can correspond with the work of the Trinity. In Hinduism while the Trimurti, Sat Cit Ananda and three Margas can correspond to the

Trinity, the context has not favoured it yet. Yet there is more positivity in this thinking as while comparing a philosophy with a faith; much creativity can be undertaken. While the ultimacy of what we follow is beyond our limited knowledge we can work with these phenomenon that have rich histories, traditions, scriptures, practices, cultures etc. rather than start from zero.

5. CREATION, SIN, SUFFERING AND SALVIFIC HISTORY

As the subject of theology leans away from the concept and operation of God we find the next stage as belonging to the human and the world. From the conception of the world and that leading into sin and suffering together with the promise, we must now discuss these aspects.

For a context such as Sri Lanka the theology of creation is not alien. Being in a resplendence of natural beauty with a majority of people involved in agriculture and not known as an industrial country; Sri Lanka shares much in line to value creation. Whether we project this as outright creation in the Bible, intelligent design etc, to an oriental nation the closeness with nature is paramount. It is no wonder that Christians celebrate all cultural festivals related to nature and also have adopted practices from nature into their faith practice. This is from celebrating the New Year festivals and the inculcation of agricultural elements to their services. There is much room to discuss ecological concerns and stewardship with the local context and Christians are able to bring their points of view as preservation of life. Buddhists may value the reality of creation even more than Christians due to the temporary abode concept. The theological questions can also be answered in the sense that evolution also can be described in terms of creationism and intelligent design. In whichever way we may view the situation, theologizing with a Buddhist and Hindu context has enriched the Christian faith and continues to do so.

The doctrine of sin, the fall and providence do not have its direct counterparts in oriental faiths. In the practical sense there is sufficient motivation to look at humanity's desperateness and disgust as to the human condition. While in a non theistic perspective sin is attributed to a person's decisions alone and in a theistic perspective to sin which had been led to this situation through a lack of Godliness and the presence temptation. In both the final result is compatible. However the causes are not, but at a closer look, both affirm that humanity is limited in this department. This also then leads into how salvation can be received. On the theistic front while this is available on the non theistic level this must be a self attempt. In the Sri Lankan context, sin has come to be known as the result of leaving faith rather than the inability to follow a faith. While temples depict heinous punishments given to the wrongful the forgiveness and metanoia are hard concepts to find in Buddhism. One issue we face with terrorism and extremism is also that the final reconciliation is always done when defeat is made and this is a good example of the lack of a 'forgiveness'. The converging point in this discussion must be placing oneself in the midst of the limitedness humanity faces but also in terms of rectification that can come from an outside source. Even the self rectification can be motivated from a higher position in whom or in which this current predicament may not lie.

Suffering is universal. And in both Christianity and in oriental faiths the concept of suffering emerges as crucial aspect of faith. While sin and suffering may not go together always, the oriental context may support it more than in the Christian faith. In Christianity the concept of suffering is always directed at a God experience and it is encouraged to embrace it in a similar manner. While in a Buddhist context the suffering can be related to karma and this continues its merry round. In this theological dilemma both religions can learn something from the other. For an example righteous and pious suffering can become part of the cultural and contextual ethic in Sri Lanka. On the other hand the idea of sin that underlines suffering in the world is a common aspect and leaves little room for the devil or any other component on which it can be blamed but solely on one's loss of dignity and discipline.

This will further the action and faith perspective in each other's religion. On a practical level, this suffering takes place across the country from rural areas to marginalized communities to those whose voicesare unheard to the many who are oppressed. There can be no theological construct to alleviate their suffering rather than by eliminating the sin that has caused them to this condition. In that regard Christian theologians emphasize more of a cause and effect process in their theological thinking against a backdrop of suffering.

The future and the hope of each religion is different. As a context of hope; has been found in the finding of peace and justice. After the mammoth destructions that we experienced from ethnic war and extremism there is not enough that can be said but that Sri Lankan growth lies when the end of violence begins. In a Christian sense the eschatological aspects all have its counterparts in the Buddhist context but with varying effect.

From a Buddhist perspective idea of Nibbana or the final extinguishing can be adapted to that of heaven and the freedom of bliss it provides. This is a workable relationship where all seek peace in this world and beyond. Theologizing in context where judgement appears on a daily basis is a new experience for Christians. While we await a time unspecified to see eschatology and the new community the Buddhist context lives it each day with the additional meaning of the eschatological event which is already in force. The hope is a constant phenomenon in the above, while in the

Christian sense it is embedded and is but spiritual hope. Praying the Lord's prayer in this context on 'Thy will be done on earth as in heaven' allows us to understand that we all become partners in the work at present. And hope for humanity whether it be in this island or all over the world is a receivable that must be done so by dedication. While the end result is different in terms of each faith we must also be humble to realize that God has indeed planted God's truth in different contexts where differences even in interpreting can be made. And this must be complementary rather than divisive.

6. CHURCH, MISSION AND SACRAMENTS

The Ashram movement became symbolic of the ecclesiology that the Indian context imparted into contextual thinking. As we mentioned in brief earlier, there are several remnants of the Ashram movement on Sri Lanka as well. These capture the interfaith and the communal aspect of the faith inculturated. This is also an indication of the churchless faith movement with ample examples of indigenization.

However in the Lankan context the understanding of the church is quite similar with that of other religious as a faith dispensation centre. In the temples structure of both the Hindu and Buddhist faiths the religious place is given paramount importance and this is actually symbolism at its best. We find many religious who flock to churches in the hope of consolation for the place rather than that of the intention.

Being a 'place' of arts and extravagant décor together with a vibe of Holiness with clergy in residence the church has become more of a religious centre in the country. This is further strengthened when we look at agricultural or plantational parishes where the church is something of a prominent meeting place. And the ecclesiological aspect of it is that of the Old Testamental understanding which is present in the church. In a way this has promoted the communal aspect in a different light and worship as well as other aspects become church centered. This allows the Church to retain its missiology in the form of gathering and tending.

Coming to the mission of the Church, when the first faithful landed on these shores the holistic mission of intellectual through schools, spiritual through churches and physical through health care became cornerstone. In the modern day this continues with education becoming central through the mission schools. The legacy of same have captured the minds of many even amidst shout of westernization and a high place is accorded to Christian education.

In terms of health care much of the institutions that 'were', have been overtaken and this has left a vacuum. However, a new reality that has even landed the church in murky waters is the idea of a rich enterprise. This is a reality in the sense that even forgoing freer churches to whom this trouble aspect in directed, even the churches in rural areas become centres where some form of assistance is delivered. Whether it comes in the form of money, food, medical or any such assistance the church has become labeled as able and possible in terms of support.

The mission of the parish locally as a prominent place of worship has been founded with the cultural elements. But with the Christian mission the place has also transformed into a place of worship. Therefore ecclesiological wise the mission of the church has been a meeting point between the two. The work of the church during the reconciliation after the war signaled that the community in the church was of the elements on the battle field, and this was due to the mixture in ethnicities and needs. The work was praiseworthy as the Church's mission was largely received well. With the mission of any religious place becoming diversified with newer ministries it is no surprise that the church will continue to bring novel concepts into this field.

The Church in Sri Lanka is very young in terms of the field of contextualization regarding worship and liturgy. This also goes for the Sacramentology that the Church brings in. While the intention of the sacraments cannot change the interpretations and the meaning itself can become profound in a cultural context. However as young maybe the Church with regard to Sacramentology, there have been some key milestones in the administration of sacraments in a liturgical sense.

The first of these can be the inculcation of the cultural elements of the wider society into faith services. These may stretch from gesture, posture and the like. The foreigner might wonder at the resplendence of symbolism within the ritualistic celebrations. The second aspect has been the risk taking element in terms of service which places the suffering of people and the interfaith context at the centre. These liturgies of the May Day mass and the New World liturgy are all very controversial variations on the theme. A third aspect can be the amalgamation of festivals locally into faith practice. By inculcatingsame the Christianity community has shown an integrated approach in their faith lives.

However the understanding of an internal grace and an external symbol can be found heavily in oriental faiths as well. This further solidifies the fact that Asian emotionalism is at play in our context. This is where we become more sentimental than our western counterparts and attach much meaning into faith acts than the more' reasoning' west. The 'feel' of the intention becomes of importance to the person in our context. That is probably why the freer church movement which caters heavily on same has made headway in the country.

A Sacramentology that caters to the hearts of people and even the non Christians are built on the rituals and customs we find in the predominant culture of the country. While critics may do their rounds on the church diluting with other religions actually what the church has integrated is merely customs. Yet the idea of a local Sacramentology has been adventurous to say the least. The effect of salvation in a mono cultural atmosphere has itself been debated and there are many aligned thinking patterns of how this works out in the present of other established faiths. The meaning of Sacramentology in this context bears much promise of further research and study as many interdisciplinary themes may emerge from same.

7. INTERFAITH THEOLOGY

While the separation of an entire chapter on interfaith theology in a short book such as this, is not necessary, the emphasis we have given to the subject is immense. And it is only in that light that we aim to present the workings of an interfaith theology in a Sri Lankan context. What must be firstly emphasized is the issue of a faith that grew up within other faiths. This underpins all what we plan and think on this issue. Secondly what we pen down here is only the version that an academia might operate in and not generally the wider church. And thirdly interfaith theology or what may seem like it, has been in operation in Sri Lanka for many years, even before the advent of the terminology. This may come as a surprise but there each Christian community and parish engages in this aspect over and over again sometime even without knowing.

Therefore what we are hoping to write here is not necessarily the lessons from the India who have progressed quite well in this arena but a new sort of thinking that stems from this context. The fear that was set upon the inhabitants by the foreign administrations was of such a tumultuous nature that any further dialogue on an interfaith level was deemed to be an end. What came about in the post independent years is not only the humbling of the Christians to acknowledge a wider culture but how well they also belonged to it. The idea of an independent governing came about with the nationalistic movements that were propagating the goodness that we shared. And in that light the church movements in a way embraced the cultural aspect.

For the church in Sri lanka the concept of a dialogue also indicated a manner in which integration and development could place. In a way it was the only way for the country to move forward. Therefore a progressive agenda included that religions do talk to each other and also in this process we learn from each other. The fine line here between being overpowered and mutual respect is acknowledged. Yet when in a minority there is enough reason for you as the minority partake the lead in this task. And what we have observed is not problematic at all. And the results of this dialogue are healthy and it has built trust. At parish level this trust converts into the developmental procedure that was discussed above.

Interfaith collaboration gives each religious community an opportunity to see each other as they are so that we do not promote emptiness in our dialogue. The manner we move forward here is the actual discussion of theological aspects and how well these have been respected in their own traditions. For many a Sri Lankan Christian the average knowledge of Hinduism and Buddhism is on a very high level. This illustrates that the learning of knowledge transpires even without our conscious wish. The context is such that we must therefore also think of our own faith in the culture that we are born into. While this is challenging, it is also an enriching exercise.

Any theological construct must be done in the intention of furthering one's on faith. This could be the point that is so often missed by evangelical thinkers. By being open to other truths we do not end up diluting our faith but by enriching the horizon and scope. At times this theological construct can take us to places that we never dream when starting out. One of the very common symbols that are given in the faith journey of people is the climbing of a mountain. And the closer you are to the top you find other people who have taken other paths. This is significant in that, that they all had the option of choosing their own path. And at the summit we all meet.

Once again in the primarily Buddhist background the fruitfulness of an interfaith theology rests heavy on how you understand a philosophy and a religion. From the merit of the fact that Buddhism does not disavow the God concept, we find Christianity in dialogue. And the moment the philosophy states its agnosticism, there is ample room to discuss about God who became a human being and promoted a lived out faith in humility to God becomes then another opening to a fruitful dialogue. Interfaith theology demonstrates that God has in time planted God's truth in different times and spaces. The attempt of a 'religious' is not only to know one, but to know as much as possible of how God operates.

What interfaith theology done in a context such as our confirms; is that pluralism is a reality. This reality is more of an advantage for the learner rather than a point of fear. The aspect of fear does not necessarily disappear when we learn about the other. But we learn accommodation based on how we also act in relation to them. The realization that we all have similar histories, traditions scriptures, customs and rituals are but heavy indications that we do have much more to learn. We become in sense elevated in our thoughts as we compare and contrast the teachings of each religion.

At the core of the argument is the question of whether you are humble enough to learn from another? Some may fear of this as they feel that the superiority of Christian faith and the 'electedness' becomes in jeopardy when we attempt this. In Interfaith theology what we endeavour to fulfill is exactly is opposite. Where we try to think of religious truth as equal in the sense that we believe it was God who has made revelation in this manner to a different context. And the context has taken this further through their limitations. And secondly we believe in the love of God that far surpasses human constructs. We become aware that our selection is also done on the basis that we love the other in whatever situation they might be. This opens not only an interfaith theological stance but it further develops our own stance. The more firm you are in your faith the more you would be able to theologically construct on an interfaith level.

8. EMERGING THEOLOGIES

While the subject of theology is increasingly becoming contextual in the Sri Lankan scenario, different newer themes have made it on to our reflection horizons. We are going to discuss these issues in details as below. There could be some debate on whether we do have a school of thought with regard to each of these theologies and whether each can be called an 'emerging' theology. Yet we are confident that these are the themes that always make the cut when we are establishing a Sri Lankan theology.

One of the prominent features in the social aspect of the country, has been the ethnic issue, war, aftermath and reconciliation. This obviously leads into many other aspects of politics, sociology and economy. There have been attempts to capture our faith in terms of this conflict and especially in the process of peace and justice. The subsequent issues have been violence, injustice, war widows, orphans and missing persons, reconstruction, healing of wounds, sacred space for sharing, painful history etc. There is much to receive from the reconciliation aspect of the New Testament towards this.

Secondly we open the gateway into the realization of the agricultural community. We also embed the experiences of daily wage labourers, housemaids in foreign countries and persons who work in the free trade zone and the like into this. The fact that these persons represent the backbone of the economy and that they still become under represented and under salaried has become a major theme in our reflections. The input on equality and recognition in the testament encourage us to reflect on these aspects.

The aspect of marginalized communities have become a commonplace term in academia. This section now encapsulates those on the margins of race, wage and voice. The communities of sexually marginalized and abused, street children, gypsies and adivasis, menial job seekers, prisoners, homeless, uneducated, the elderly etc. The issue with regard to these communities is multiple.

They do not hold a particular context on which their situation suffers but with the perception in the eyes of the 'other' this phenomenon takes place. The parables and the stories of Jesus in his outreach to the neglected in those communities hold much support in the theological task within these communities. There has also been efforts to address these issues through the social change that place through Diaconal ministry.

As the country has maintained its religious thrust as one where people consider religion to be of great use, the story of a unified Church has been a goal for many decades. With several attempts that were undertaken by the protestant church and the many schemes that were resolved, the dream of same has been one on a rough path. In addition to this we also the work of the Roman Catholics as being a heavy majority yet with their stance firmly exclusive it has become necessary to challenge their take on ecumenism. Equally on the other side we find an aggressive and some time ignorant Free Church alliance that has also held exclusivity and has become a point of departure rather than unity. When considering this, it not only proves of the need for an ecumenical theology but also a theology that in which many members have ownership. In the prayers of Jesus and the books of Paul we find much consolation towards this ownership. In recent times there have also been attempts of both the extremes to marginalize the rest which has eroded the unified message to the wider context. The work must then be of our theologizing task to go forward positively in the hope that churches will adhere to their call for unity.

While being a very new player in terms of industrialization and technology, the country whose natural beauty was the envy of many, Sri Lanka continues to face ecological issues where a tug of war ensues that we depart from an agricultural setting. This push against environment exploitation has become the result of policy and politics. In a way we have been unable to stand firm in the policy of an agricultural nation and the investments have become politicized. Investments here are referred to projects and use of land for varied purposes. The ecological concerns in the Bible coming from an Asian perspective resound heavily to our context as well. In this regard out theologizing must focus on a developing nation but with a modern outlook and above all, respect and dignity towards God's world.

The case of Secularism maybe gradual in the sense of all countries and especially in a country such as ours where religion takes a prominent place, this topic might not be discussed at length. But owing to the philosophical and ethical standing of Buddhism there is ample room for a majority to be nominally religious. This has become prominent in the west where only a few seem to hold fast onto their faiths. In the same time this gives rise into extremism of those who may not want this gradual decline of religion. They are more concerned that the only hope of resuscitation of faith must be through the fundamental approach. As secularization and extremism have shown their destructive paths in the recent path, theologizing within these contexts becomes challenging. The faith vs reason aspect that dominates this discussion must face the accountability of the Bible in both testaments. New gospel and culture approaches have been discussed where faith search goes on even in the marketplace. While not as much as the west may do so as they are affected more with it, the Asian context also makes inroads into this. As far as extremism goes this sensitive issue with politics, psychology and education imbued into it, the theologizing framework can must align itself with the many current challenges of the context.

9. CURRENT THINKERS

This essay has taken into consideration all the work, interest and scholarship that have been attempted by modern Sri Lankan theologians. While the output canbe different than that of a theological academia in an advanced setting, this writing goes on with the spirit of how things can turn up with time and expertise.

The expertise here is accounted firstly by any studies that the person has undertaken over the years regarding the subject. Secondly with publications, each person is called to present their continually as it is the best possible manner in which the ideas of a contextual theology takes shape. And thirdly the engagements in teaching which can be done at the Theological College as well as in other institutions become valid for the acceptance as a scholar in the given subject area.

We start with Biblical studies and following the work of Leslie Dareeju, Rajeev Palihawadana and Christopher Balraj have done studies in relation to the Old

Testament. On the side of the New Testament following Muthiah Selvaraj, Kandiah Karunasekera, ShanthakumarSureshkumar, Jyothini Seenithamby, Lionel Peiris are the main thinkers on this line. On the Historical front following the work of Stephen Arulampalam, Jayasirir Peiris and G Somaratna who has also specialized in the theology of disability can be highlighted. Their work stretches from the exegesis of Testamental books into the relating of same into modern crisis. This stream has become vital as the earlier mentioned re-reading is attempted through this and a Sri Lankan glimpse can be achieved when much material becomes present in this regard.

In terms of Christian communication the following work of Alfred Jebanesan, the work of Nishantha Fernando, Nimal Wickremaratne, Jayanth Paditharatne can be considered as essential in this arena. In liturgy Lakshman Daniel, Narmasena Wicramasinghe, Marc Billimoria have led this field. In music we have Lakpriya De Silva, Ravishankar Niles and Joshua Ratnamwho have made noteworthy contributions. When considering Religions the works of Mahendran, Selvanathan Selvan and Shelton Daniel are of noteworthy mention who is also interested in Christian education. Wasana Fernando has also taken the lead in this latter field. The work of Anandaraj, Jerome Annan and Sisters of Methpiyasa can also be discussed as vital for the Ashram movement in Sri Lanka. This section has been predominantly affected by the arts, literature, worship and music as has been mentioned. With the local culture firmly embedded in this section of faith practice, most of our identity has been placed in high acceptance when considering localized theology. The presence of this field is becoming extremely vital in the process of identification.

In terms of Counseling we have Anburaj and Mahesh Hemachandra who have led this discipline. The latter has also worked on ecumenism which was mentioned earlier as field of necessary intervention. In terms of womanist thinking the work of Kamalam Joel can be described as essential. On theological and related fields the newest addition of diakonia and management has been done by Nadaraja Arulnathan while a similarly work is attempted by Vathsala Paulraj. In terms of theological studies following Rienzie Perera, Danushka Dilshan, Lakmal Panditharatne, are the new generation with regard to this emphasis while Nishantha Gunaselera and Hasitha Fernando are also motivated in this regard. In sociological terms the work of Keerthisiri Fernando can be mentioned with emphasis on integration while Jerome Sahabandu has also captured the essence in this field. In Conflict Management the work of Somasiri Perera, Anura Perera and Saman Perera are mentioned. With emphasis on a wider angle of theological areas, contextual theology comes to life through these elements. It is no secret that contextual theology becomes of great use when done interculturally. In a context such as Sri Lanka the resources are abundant to make sure that what we promote in has a strong reference to the localize setting.

The work of the Theological College of Lanka's Journal must also have special mention here as much theological thinking has become possible through this forum. The essays stretch from Biblical material to Mission centered theology. It has worldwide circulation and has captured the essence of Sri Lanka theology. The issue so language is also mentioned here as when the College became a Swabasha College, the effort in the use of local language was emphasized. However, without the formation in English this trend of expressing in English has decline and this has made a vacuum in what the outside world can fathom from us.

There are two other publications namely, Sandeepani and Vidivei Nokki in the local languages which captures much more in poetry, prose, idiom and culture yet the translation of same has not taken place. Therefore, while the predicament of learning theology in local languages is present but without much material, the theologizing task is left in an alienated state. The issue of language is not uncommon. It affects almost all third world countries who want to speak from their language but also into a foreign academia. Mostly the established academia is receptive to the intention of this task but on a practical sense this becomes difficult as they are unable to work in two mediums. This has kept indigenized theologies at bay throughout their expansion and becomes of interest as a footnote in wider academia. With the introduction of contextual theology and interdisciplinary studies a mainstay, this phenomenon of language might receive its recognition it deserves.

In the field of current thinking in contextual thinking, most of whattranspires is not captured in terms of 'scholarly' articles or books. Where most contextual thinking takes place is at forums, local newspapers, occasional liturgies, hymns and arts. While a concentrated effort has yet been undertaken to collate all of these it is necessary to do so in the hope of a realistic contribution. Especially at the Theological college the effort of localizing theology is visible with creeds, liturgies and composition in the arts. On the basis of the college becoming a lab of experimentation the works would remain forever lost. Therefore with the advent of modern archiving and translation it is much hoped that the future of a Sri Lankan theology will be made vibrant, accessible and far reaching.

10. THE FUTURE OF SRI LANKAN THEOLOGY

The future of any academia stays strong on three important aspects. These are people, resources and processes. In a Sri Lankan scenario, with its academia relatively young and with a hope that can stretch a long way, we are confident that all the above three aspects would fall inline as time progresses.

To start developing on the first aspect, the dearth in theological studies at a higher level has been dire when comparing with other established fields. For just over seven decades the number of doctorates produced can be counted with two palms. And some of these have become domiciled abroad. The fact that higher studies are looked upon as a stepping stone has enriched the chance of many for higher positions in the Church and this has inevitably dampened the chance of them who will teach further or engage in research. From a personal view point even when a person is called to act in such a manner in studies but become unhinged based on the temptations that surround, it is only reasonable that they fall by the wayside in term of an academic. Another important aspect in this story has been capacity building. The level for studies at a European standard is quite benchmarked. It calls for persons in terms of language, skill, commitment and capacity. Unfortunately with a pastoral setup mainly in churches there seem to be no end in the struggle a person undergoes in being able to fulfill these skills. And when you are at an age of 40 the church finally may release them for same. But in terms of academics this is a ripe old age and the contributory factor for them in terms of years has become past.

The second aspect as mentioned above is resources. The idea of resource in this regard is that availability of options for furthering the discipline. This can stretch from books, to courses to seminars to study options, language development and will of the policy makers. While most of these in Sri Lanka remain at an underprivileged level there can be a few bright lights seen in a distance. One of these is the development of the net capacity and accessibility. Through this more online versions can be found linking to studies that were certainly not possible a few decades back. Even on the front of the availability of courses while the west has closed a few doors, there seem to be a modern wave in the southern hemisphere and also with interculturism there is more opportunities even at the western level to be part of larger faculties. In terms of the upskilling or capacity building more effort has been put in, and there is sufficient data to support that these have been received well by prospective scholars.

While it is unequal when considering the opportunities available to each denomination a more level playing field is made possible with the intervention of Theological College. Also with regard to resources we are now able to attract more foreign scholars as well in the task of exchange. It also goes into show that this region has become a curious case that is in need of study along with other similar locations. While the foreign input was always present there in terms of study and research the opportunities have increased and widened. There is also opportunity for translation of resources at a higher level which improves the workability of the expression from the local context. To cite one example would be the e-media where easily the local essence can be given succinctly and circulated widely.

When we come to process as a component, in terms of the Sri Lankan theological academia we find advancements that have taken place to develop same. On the one hand there is the process of training people for same. There seem to be a political will that has come from all protestant denominations that calls for an urgent need to train and develop scholars. The motivation is a little short of a competition. However we leave some room to finalize the result of this motivation as whether it is church led and mission centered or person led and career centered. In the long run with many persons engaging in same the academia is surely to benefit. On the other hand when we look at process we also look at the availability of lay study. One of the main emphasis of a budding academia is that its shared. In some cases it can also be the future of all theological academia. Once again the Sri Lankan context is but a long distance behind in this regard. However, the policy of the Theological college has become skewed in this manner that they are now open for scholarship in whichever way possible. In terms of theological scholarship the academia has also encouraged publication from both lay and clergy. While the output of same has been dismal to say the least, individuals have become motivated to take part in this process. In a way one challenge for protestant mainline academia is the emergence of freer church colleges. These do not conform to the normal rigidity of scholarship but also provide much drive in terms of output and presence. While this has spurred the mainline academia the results of same will take many years to be noticed.

While we did focus on people, process and resources there is still much out there, on which the future of this select academia reviles upon. In the western world interdisciplinary work has becomes key in such discussions. The contribution towards the secular world is also becoming pivotal. In Sri Lanka this academia is relatively young and we might also add at a blossoming stage. The blossom must be adequately supported both by the Church as policy makers but also by congregations at all levels. Unless we determine to give prominence the art and the science of it will suffer a power shortage. It is our hope that this may not be an occurrence.

Appendices

CONTEXTUALIZATION: THE STORY OF THE DIOCESE OF KURUNAGALA PART I

This is an attempt to capture the factors that have influenced the Diocese of Kurunagala[1] in adapting cultural practices and promoting indigenous worship in the life of her ministry.

Geographical Argument

The Diocese of Kurunagala the missionary diocese of the Church of Ceylon [2] came into being in 1950. The geographical location or the carving of the Diocese out of the larger Diocese of Colombo is an interesting case which relates to the discussion of contextualization.

It is made up of the six provinces out of the nine in the island. These provinces also make claim to the ancient

---

[1]http://dioceseofkurunegala.com/
[2]https://www.anglicancommunion.org/structures/member-churches/member-church/diocese.aspx?church=ceylon&dio=colombo

Kingdoms of the country. Starting from Anuradhapura, Polonnaruwa, Kurunagala and Matale as well as Kandy which was the last monarchical Kingdom in the country[3].

The significance of being carved in to the ancient kingdom suggests that the areas which comprise also captured the cream of the cultural practice at that time. This could be from art to architecture as well as from food to attire. This does make the case that even religion which is practiced in the region becomes cultural.

When we look at language we see that save for a very few all the parishes in the Diocese of Kurunagala work in the local languages. This is in contrast to the Colombo counterpart which was influenced more by the Society for the propagation of the gospel. In most of these parishes we find English being used as a working language.

---

[3]http://lakdiva.org/codrington/sovereigns.html

Two organizations are recognized as missionary entities which comprised the Diocese of Kurunagala. These were the Church Missionary Society which undertook their mission in the rural villages and the Tamil Church Mission which worked in the plantation sectors.

It is possible that both these movements targeted more of the labourer and farmer communities within the Diocese and the catechists that worked with them found it easier to use the local idiom and culture as vehicle for their evangelical task.

The adorning with 'Sesath' or Fans and 'Hella' or Spears invite the congregation to think of the altar as the reception room of the King who made audience with the locals in the bygone era.

Similarly in the Thamil speaking areas the use of a long handled pan to burn incense on important occasions symbolize the similar instrument the Hindu devotees use to circle in front of different gods in awe and worship.

This is much cultural rather than the elaborate thurible used in modern times.

Apart from these we see many of the chants in tune and language being inculcated in liturgies which were commonplace in folklore, when working in paddy fields, when going on long journeys, when travelling by boat, when staying awake to protect harvests from animals and tunes which were used in village games.

The Independence Movement argument

It is difficult to look at the Diocese without mentioning the first Bishop the Rt RevdLakdasa De Mel. However we look at his contribution to the Diocese, which shook off his roots within the English educated atmosphere with the lens of the times of the country.

In 1950 leading into the 70's was a period of great change within the country[4]. In one way it was the breaking away from the colonial past but also itlead into

---

[4]https://www.britannica.com/place/Sri-Lanka/Growth-of-nationalist-power

a vacuum which was to be filled up with the indigenous resources, thinking, potential etc.

Bishop Lakdasa was in a way influenced by these happenings and on top of the fact of being in a cultural geographical location he also insisted that the Church becomes one with the National Ideology. His famous saying as it goes was '"We are not only Ceylonese Christians, but we are also Christian Ceylonese. If Ceylon goes up, we go up with her. We will never desert Ceylon."

With almost all the foreign theological colleges being distanced in 1963 a decision was taken of initiating the Theological College of Lanka in Pilimatalawa. It was to be a 'Swabahsa' or local language college. From the chapel to the language of instruction to the celebration of local festivals with a Christian interpretation it was a significant step in the direction of the nationalism that was infusing with the times and Bishop Lakdasa as someone who was in the thick of things was a pioneer architect in same.

The prayer book in 1970 which was a Sinhala translation saw am attempt of using the local terminology to denote theological and ecclesiological concepts. While the Inculturation movement would not have had much legal leeway within the major constitutions of the Church of England we can observe minute details which have been incorporated into liturgies. One example of this is the 'Jaya Mangala Gatha' [5] a Pali and then Sinhala poem of blessing which has got incorporated in Christianity in marriage liturgies.

Due respect much also be paid to the second Bishop of the Diocese who took this further by incorporating cultural aspects from both Sinhala and Thamil cultures. Some of his initiatives were the using of drums and Nadaswaram[6] in procession which were used to lead processions for the King or Queen in an ancient time. This was a break away, even from that time from

---

[5]https://dhammawiki.com/index.php/Jaya_Mangala_protection_verses_(English_and_Pali)
[6]https://en.wikipedia.org/wiki/Nadaswaram

motorcades or horses which preceded royalty or the rulers of the crown. This was significant in the fact that it spelled a new order of royalty which was now being recognized.

In a way the non Roman Catholic Church at large was in search for is identity after nationalism slowly tightened its screws around the prestige the Church held in the time between independence and the pre-capitalism era in the late 80's. Therefore it is natural that the Church had to mix with the cultural aspect of the country to be appealing and at the same time surviving.

The Multi Cultural Argument

The Asian context is pluralistic with religiosity but also with other monasticisms, mysticisms, movements and spiritualities. And top of it religion is a factor of great importance to the people in Sri Lanka as give in this statistic. [7]

---

[7]https://en.wikipedia.org/wiki/Importance_of_religion_by_country

We can see the influence especially of Buddhism and Hinduism in several faith aspects in the Diocese of Kurunagala. When we go back to the initiatives by Bishop Lakdasa we see his contribution in the formation of the monastic order at Devasaranaramaya[8]. This was the attempt by Sevaka (servant) Yohan Devananda to initiate discussion between Buddhist, Christian and Marxist ideologies. Bishop Lakshman was also a pioneer in this movement[9] however he was more drawn to it as a justice based issue.

The following Affirmation of Faith is adapted from the 'New World Liturgy' Sevaka Yohan experimented with in his time at Devasaranaramaya.

We acknowledge our responsibility for sin and evil, in the world, in our country, in our work places, in our homes and schools, in our temples and churches.

---

[8] https://dioceseofcolombo.lk/the-ceylon-churchman/archive/april-june.../searchtext.swf

[9] https://www.colombotelegraph.com/index.php/my-memories-of-the-rt-revd-lakshman-wickremesinghe-1927-1983/

We acknowledge our want of faith, hope and love. We acknowledge our pride, vanity and self indulgence.

We acknowledge our selfishness and narrowness of spirit and our exploitation of others. We acknowledge our failures and omissions in the care and service of others. We acknowledge divisions among us, and failures and omission in corporate action for justice for the oppressed.

We need cleansing and forgiveness and humility of spirit. We need new life, true community and real joy. We need liberation, reconciliation and peace.

Silence

We seek to change our lives and to change the organisation of society. In order to help build a new society and a new humanity, a new heaven and a new earth.

We seek a revolution of mind and spirit, a revolution in the structures of society, a revolution in the human relationships between leaders and people, administrators and workers, teachers and pupils, parents and children, priests and laity. We seek liberation of all those who are oppressed. We see to commit ourselves to the struggle for liberation.

We seek a new order of love, justice and peace that all may care. We seek sharing of power and resources, of leadership and responsibility. We seek day by day to translate principles into practice as far as we can, alongside the people according to dharma[10].

The text is dwells on 'suffering' from all the three aspects mentioned above and it talks of alleviation of suffering from also the three respective perspectives. It was liturgy in which all many could participate affirming their preference but also learning from the other.

The practice of 'Thai Pongal' a festival of new beginnings and thanking the Sun has been in practice interpreted by many congregations in the Diocese as a harvest festival with praise for God's creation of the environment. The red sash shown below wrapped around

---

[10]https://www.uspg.org.uk/docstore/146.pdf

a coconut husk as in Hinduism is most times replaced by a cross.

Here it is also important to notice that when we look at Buddhism and Hinduism the former is a philosophy rather than a religion and the latter is known as an umbrella religion which encompasses almost any spiritual interpretation. Therefore it is with the flow that Christians are able to accommodate their faith in collaboration with these ideologies.

CONTEXTUALIZATION: THE STORY OF THE DIOCESE OF KURUNAGALA PART 2

In the first part of this series, we looked at how contextualization took place within the Diocese in the past 70 years. In this article we will see two other aspects of how contextualization in faith has come about in our journey.

The first example comes to us from the Panideniya chapel symbolized as the identity of Sri-Lankan building architecture. The full story of the chapel as related by its minister in charge, can be found in this link. https://m.facebook.com/story.php?story_fbid=15601452 14141091&id=100004368814927?sfnsn=mo&d=n&vh= i

He describes the history of the chapel with the consecration in 1927 close to a century of years ago. He continues to discuss the marvels of this building which brings together the local heritage in the form of architecture. These elements of stone and wooden designs are only paralleled by the historical Ambekke buildings. This presentation also includes as to why the builders chose to present this chapel in this form rather leaving the traditional setup. The actual inculturation model of royalty for divinity is made visible through these characteristics to immerse the congregation in awe within their own local setting. Set out to be the centre of spiritual nurture of the Training College it remains to be an embodiment of how we in the Diocese view gospel in culture.

Secondly as the Vesak season comes upon us during an almost closed society due to the crisis, we see a scaled down celebration of the intention within our parishes. A festival of light, is symbolized in the Vesak lanterns that adorn the Church of the Living Christ decorated glamorously.

Again we see the symbol of light reflected on the walk to the church in Aragoda whose saints were commemorated on 1st May. The diocese and hence the congregation participate in these adornments not merely to stand in solidarity with another festival of a different faith. But it is done consciously to signify recognition and the connection we make with the liberation elements in faiths. This is understood as 'intertwined pluralism' in interfaith dialogue.

The cathedral has alsays been a centre of cultural enhancement and the Dan Sala of this season has achived quite some populality. Here we see how the symbolic light is offered in the relation to to Jesus' message of 'you are the ligth of the world' and that a 'light cannot be hidden'. God who brings light to the world and makes the 'lgiht shine in darkenss' is venerated with the presentation of lamps.

In the past article we witnessed how local festivities such as Thail Pongal and the Sinhala/Thamil new year become enshrined as cultural symbolisms in faith transmission. We as a Diocese together with subsequent Bishops in their 'reach for the mission within the context' cherished these 'meeting points' to further elaborate that faith does not occur in a vacuum and by enriching faith in culture we become more realistic of what how our mission needs to be interpreted.

CONTEXTUALIZATION: THE STORY OF THE DIOCESE OF KURUNAGALA PART 3

In part one under this topic we looked at the basic liturgical aspects that the Diocese inherited from the context it was given birth to and in the second installment we looked at architecture and local festivals which have been interpreted in an indigenous light.

As the Diocese of Kurunagala continues to commemorate the 70th anniversary of establishment in this issue we look at the 'village parish' in cultural setting. The rural village and the plantation are not far away from the ministerial centre in the Diocese. To exactly pin point to a percentage, $4/5^{th}$ or 80% of the parishes in the Diocese are in a non urban setting.

Reflecting upon this fact in the context of urbanization that has taken place across the country, it is an amazing detail. This amazing fact inevitably governs the way we think, act, reflect and practice faith.

It is indeed a calming feeling to take a stroll in one of the uncarpeted roads which leads to a village parish. You are met with smiling faces and at all times well known faces. The environs are clean, devoid of pollution and if on hillsides met with cooling air. The horseback missionaries themselves would have found another world in these calm settings as opposed to cities where much action was taking place!

The village parishes were always small in nature expect for the one which have been expanded in recent years. These are always situated in the midst of a rather large field or property. Thus signifies that when the missionaries were in operation they had allocated larger estates for their service but with churches as mission centers. Almost all of these parishes are unable to hold all the congregation if all chooses to attend the service at a specific time.

The 'closeness' of the parishioners, marks a very unique feature in this setup. A bell rung announcing a death or the start of a service is physically capable of gathering all the families in the village who all reside within earshot. The Work of the church is not dissimilar to that of the work of the temple in a village. The same reverence is given the places of worship with the calmness and serenity of the vicinity. The attire and the removal of shoes both signify this to a greater aspect. It is uncommon to see children and adults attending church if not garbed in a white dress.

The oil lamps always take precedence over candles and mats over carpets with Sesath a common occurrence. The 'local' instruments still accompany services, although in the recent time the electric organ has also made inroads. One area the village parishes still hold dear is certainly the use of the indigenous hymn books. It is reassuring to know that almost all of these hymns and not only a few keep occurring in a non rural parish throughout the year. It is no secret that surrounded by the resplendence of the natural beauty most of these literature was penned down.

There is always some sort of garden produce that is offered during the offertory. This practice even not in the offertory setting was prevalent for a long period in the history of the Diocese as this is often looked upon with a different light than the usual offertory mindset. It is more of sustenance of the clergy that is being shared within the community but which is offered as thanksgiving to God. Meals are also on a roster which is likened to the food sharing in a Buddhist temple whose recipient monks are cared for by the community. In an even starker similarity some rural areas continue to use the address style of monks to Christian clergy! This maybe the best the incarnation ideology offer to the Christian missions that became inculcated in context rather than were poured down from a different context.

The village parish, unlike in an urban setting, is a hub of activity throughout the year. The closeness that was mentioned above could be the reason for this or it would simple mean that the church is not far from the life of the people. Parishioners continue to practice visiting clergy for writing letters and the interpretation of correspondence. There is much respect for seniority and the tale of persons who take delight in reciting these over and over again of how each family helped build up the parish are of legend. It points once again to a local Buddhist/Hindu interpretation which governs religious relationships where elders are always found to be the flag bearers of the 'tradition' within the parish context.

The parishes continue to be hubs of activity at local festivals. It is almost mandatory as it seems for everyone in the village to participate in the feast of the Church. The pandals that come up are always the work of an integrated movement. Similarly the April New Year is celebrated with much cultural elements in the parish. This includes the sports, decorations and the food. The harvest festivals both at the parish and the village levels are important occasions. The paddy field itself is associated heavily as a cultural symbol and post harvest, a place of gathering and even at times a setting for Christmas carols.

It is a blessing to have this unique culture embedded in the Diocese's DNA so to speak. It is not prone to immunity in this time where modern trends are making inroads in to how we act and reflect. It is important to note that they themselves of the village parishes are proud of this heritage and they do everything to conserve this goodness. These institutions continue to play a vital role in the 'say' they have in the Diocese's ministry of incarnation. And it is something that the Church in the global space can also appreciate and use as a canvass in the ongoing dialogue of gospel and culture.

CONTEXTUALIZATION: THE STORY OF THE DIOCESE OF KURUNAGALA PART 4

The attempt of accommodating the idea of contextualization into four compartments has been challenging. More than what has been said, the mind wanders to what has not been mentioned or what could not make the 'cut' to fit into this reflection. In part one we discussed on the sociological, geographical and economical aspects in the story of the Diocese of Kurunagala.

In the second installment prominence was given to the arts, aesthetics, customs, festivals and the rituals. In the third, we were able to discuss the local church in the village and the plantation with its own uniqueness, touched upon by the fresh breeze and its general life within it. In the fourth section while the contenders are many some idea of the interfaith collaboration must be mentioned as with the celebration of the seventieth year this aspect has been a mainstay of consideration and influence within the Diocese.

Sri Lanka had all its current religious faiths imported. However, the coming of Christianity was relatively late than the other great religious traditions. And with its arrival in the form of foreign rule and missionary activity, its impact has been felt on all spheres of life in the country.

Different than coming from a mono- religious faith context, the experience of being a new faith in the multitude of other faiths is novel. It calls not for enforcing one's own faith in the context but rather an inclusive approach of symbiosis. This is being in a 'lived out' faith journey with those who may not belong to our faith and being nourished both ways.

The Diocese of Kurunagala has maintained a very positive stance with regard to interfaith dialogue and interfaith relations. The emphasis on 'very' is stressed upto the level that some proponents within the national church, even going to the level of being critical, for its wider ecumenical outlook. The Diocese of

Kurunagalawas carved especially to work with people of other faiths in harmony, owing to the agricultural and plantations settings of the Diocese where a majority of our neighbours belong to Buddhist ad Hindu faiths.

It is a well known fact that the Anglican Communion mechanizes on the five marks of mission. In our reflections we have added a further element to make it six; whereby we recognize interfaith collaboration as a further addition. This could be related to the work of the general Anglican church in Sri Lanka but specifically due to the understanding of the work of the Diocese in the cultural geography in Sri Lanka spanning the late Kingdoms where faith and culture was preserved to make its mark. The practice of this mission extends from interfaith forums and action at the highest level in the national sphere to the mutual invitation we receive and extend at the local parish level. Occasions of ministers being addressed in the Buddhist terminology of priests is not rare, and from the practice of the New Year, Vesak, Dansal, removing of footwear upon entry, sitting on the ground, idioms, customs, rituals stretch to a long line of many, many aspects which influence is felt in a profound manner.

To cite a few examples from the recent past, extremist attacks on churches in Sri Lanka, extremist attacks on Muslims, the Tsunami, the aftermath of the civil war, all had interfaith components which were led by Anglican ambassadors in the hope of peace, harmony justice and cooperation. In the Diocese of Kurunagala at the neighbourhood level parishes are called to invite religious dignitaries from other faiths for occasions, events, festivals and collaborative tasks. The syllabuses of Anglican and for that matter all mainline church ministers, have a special branch of study titled "Religion and Society" where each aspect of our neighbour's faith is respected, studied and recognized. This makes sure that ministers realize that other faiths are but partners in mission and not adversities. There are occasions where Christian ministers are presented with titles in Buddhist terminology and tradition that elevates them into respect within their faith ranks. And this maybe a surprising story to many persons who may not have realize the depth of the relationship faiths share in this context.

Sri Lanka continues to be a religious oriented country, in that religions mean a lot to everyone. It was ranked in the top five countries where people were convinced that religions played a major role in their lives. In that regard, the wonderful tapestry of religious harmony and cooperation that has been modeled through the ages must be held with high importance. There are two main reasons for this. The first is the ability that this model provides for harmonious coexistence. In a country where people look up to religious leaders it is necessary that they promote this ideology as one that is pro-life giving. The second is witness to them who are not like us and also witness to the wider world. Even in the case that my brother and sister may not want to dialogue with me; I must take the initiative to dialogue with him or her.

Our world is witness to many conflicts that have raged because of the differences in our faiths. Yet we all believe that the ultimate reality of God bypasses all our human limitedness and understanding. In this regard, if God has accepted, then there is no reason why we can decline to dialogue with our neigbhour who may have a different faith. In Sri Lanka and in the Diocese we have not come to this conclusion based on theory or frameworks. But this has come down to us through experience. While both these terms of interfaith dialogue and interfaith relations are relatively new concepts from a first world context, the workings of same have been part and parcel of life in the Asian culture even through centuries.

Therefore, the Diocese remains committed for the development and collaboration between faiths. We feel that as we are called to proclaim the reign of God, we do so when we accept and work with our neighbours. While we realize that in the modern world, this topic maybe toxic amidst varied issues, God calls us in Jesus who broke down barriers and opened the way of liberation to all. As we remember and pray for all efforts of interfaith peace and harmony in the world, may God's guidance, patience, wisdom and peace be upon us all.

FACETS OF RECONCILIATION: A DIOCESAN PERSPECTIVE

Introduction

When the Diocese of Kurunegala of the Church of Ceylon took shape in 1950 it was both an exciting and an adventurous initiative. It was a total step in the unknown and hence the two words of exciting and adventurous, as many would have weighed the positives and the negatives of the whole venture. This articulation on the topic above becomes itself an exciting and adventurous task as it seeks to present the concept of 'reconciliation' in a more broader kaleidoscopic sense based on the history of the Diocese.

The history of the Diocese also becomes the history of post colonial Sri Lanka and this aspect will be adequately dealt with in the paragraphs to follow. Reconciliation as it will be used almost elsewhere in this issue deriving from Christian and Biblical roots will be presented towards the latter of this article especially when we shall see the current trends for reconciliation from a grass root level. This article claims to be very specific almost on the lines of a case study concentrating on a certain region of the island and in no way expressive of the macro level picture of the greater phenomenon of conflict and reconciliation.

Reconciling the 'Foreigness' of the Christian Church
It could be a mere consequence as to the apt time period when the Diocese of Kurunegala actualized, as it was the same time frame when the Sri Lankan identity sought root in the localness of the country. The architect behind the carving of the diocesan boundaries Bishop Lakdasa De Mel, who being exposed to the richness of the local Church and his passion for the indigenous life style took on that most bold initiative by using demarcation, in order to realize a faith practice within the local culture reconciling the foreign with the local.

The history student would no doubt agree that out of all the religious traditions that came into Sri Lanka the Christian faith was the foremost when it comes, to where the superiority of the adherents was used as 'the' tool in the conquering process. The use of inferiority in the colonization procedure by the westerners is a fact that not only affected the Indian subcontinent but was more of a generality all over the world rather than the exception. When the foreign rule came towards extinguishment the spark of 'love for culture' drew into such a massive furnace that it gorged everything in the path that stood against it including education, language, employment, social strata and even the Christian faith itself. The path of destruction left initially by the westerners proclaiming a more 'conquering Christ' and the next by the majoritarian Buddhists proclaiming a 'resurgent nationalism' had to be reconciled. This effort was largely lost on many fronts but if at all pacified it could be traced to the makings of this particular Diocese.

Reconciling with the Foreigness of Policies

Under its first Bishop the Sinhalese culture, traditions, language and attitudes became much imbibed into all aspects of faith administration. It was an attempt to show that the faith that was received via westerners could be practiced without 'westerness'. While worship, policies, relationships with Buddhist factions, local festivals and administration became toned down to 'go with the flow' of the time it was a balancing act which left little space for error. Under the second Bishop the Thamil culture was also given much impetus. It was during this particular time that left party movements became prominent in the country and the overall libertarian view of social life became a centre of focus. Rt. Revd. Lakshman Wickremasinghe played a key role in the attempt to workout reconciliation from the Church between oppressive policies both economically and politically and the opposition that had built up against same.

This inculturation was embraced in such a manner that even the outsider who walks into a diocesan church especially in the village and the hills will be deeply moved by the aroma of indigenization. As such reconciliation was taking place on a religious front the social reconciliation was continued by the infusing of Church participation in the socialist movement. The community of the Diocese of Kurunegala belonged in numbers to the working class, and the open economical activities enticed the more conservatively held econo-politic flow to drive towards a capitalist nature and the social movement of the Diocese was but one giant step in path of the reconciling process.

Reconciling Spiritualities

A monastic movement had begun in the diocese symbolizing the value of a simple life. It is also the period of the spiritualities which revolve around the Pentecostal movement and the prosperity gospel. Reconciliation between spiritualities becomes a matter of conscience and it is difficult to state how the Church faced it head on. The third Bishop of the Diocese Rt. Revd. Andrew Kumarage's life and ministry becomes of vital important to us at this juncture. His model of inner spirituality became a reflection which assisted in the process of such reconciliation. We have come to the early eighties in which the open wounds of the ethnic conflict has taken its roots. Many villages in the Diocese had youth battling on open fields as tensions escalated and agreements fell between political holds. Ethic communities worshiping in the same Church would have itself become a challenge to the faithful during these times. The fear of the 'other' became a feature which could not be hidden for anytime longer. Political agendas made the Christian Sinahalese majority in the Diocese decide on belonging to their creed or to their 'own'. The Indian Thamil wording in the birth certificates of the minority Christian community made them decide on aligning with creed or their 'own'. It is for this very matter that inner spirituality became the need of the hour to work at coexisting at the ground level. The training of ministers during these periods revolved around the training of spiritualities as well. As spiritualities emerged though the conflict of theological reasoning reconciling between each became an important tool in the arsenal of the prospective minister.

Subsequently the reconciliation ethic under the next three Bishops of the Diocese, took on the wholesome nature of what is defined by scholars as reconciliation. The Diocese at the turn of this century was in the predicament of voicing for the injustices of certain communities that faced backlash with the ethnic tensions. This was a calling that was heeded well in a Diocese which has representatives from both ethnicities. The diocese was in a practical reconciliation mode as they tried to speak up for the rights lost and peace that was formed in terms without justice. The reconciliation at this stage was directed at the suffering of the many in terms of a prolonged conflict and the extremisms that were not sympathetic towards either of these. The next stage belonged to the aftermath of the ethnic conflict. Here there was a divisive stand between two strands of thinking.

While the Diocese did not necessarily envisage the taking part of either, there were tendencies that made the Diocese part of both these thinking. It was in one way directed at a reconciliation that was forced and in line with peace without justice. On the other it was a battle for the soul of truth and righteousness. The reconciliation at this time was between paths of reconciliation itself. It was also during this time that elections came about and changed the populist motion of governance in the country. With this the structure of governance changed and a new era was born, however it was not to last long. The same progressive elements did die soon enough and once again a going back was expected. In the present context a major discussion point has been on identities that have come about and how these lead into conflict. There is ample evidence to show that reconciling between identities, hard as it may seem can be a solution to the situation at hand. While we look forward to the next era of change, hopefully a diocese that was carved especially for reconciliation will be of witness to the outside world and especially to the general population in the country.

Current Trends

As a jubilee of years passed from the inception of the Diocese the country saw the heightening and the dwindling of the conflict. Reconciliation today has become a house hold concept. This current issue of the SLJTR also celebrates a variation on the same theme. It has become a topic of creative theologizing as well as a promise screamed from platforms. In the outer world away from Christian Theologizing varied parties find the current push for reconciliation a mere mock. Global focus groups, local political entities and the like find the word reconciliation related with much more baggage as overpowering, assimilation and the like. In the same way an even larger entity seem to support the current reconciliation trend as noble and effective. The Christian Church in Sri Lanka, based on general standpoints is also divided on the issue, and battles rage through from arguments at minor meetings through to press releases. Once again standing true to the idea of this article it is necessary not to view the reconciliation phenomenon on a macro scale but at the ground level as experienced throughout the Diocese.

It is in order to state a few of these challenges that affect reconciliation. The use of media throughout the island has become a very strong factor in determination of the concept of reconciliation. While totally varied interpretations flow across media channels it remains whether the common citizen is able to identify the multi faces of the same phenomenon. When referring to the

Diocese it is even more suitable to mention that many of the faithful still remain away from cities and therefore away from global technology which in a way streamlines the information they receive. This in turn becomes a tool with which thinking outside a given frame becomes impossible. Next the effect of politicization needs to be mentioned as in developing countries it becomes a great force especially powered on by the people who themselves lack power economic or otherwise.

Therefore in low economic situations politicization hold the power to sway minds of individuals and groups towards a stated norm and prevents any opposition towards it. This stands evident when relating it to this geographical region. When discussing of the modern challenges a most positive factor is also education. It is quite apparent that generations which grew in the context of hate and violence for the most part have not been able to erase deeper emotions towards the 'other'. In the modern education system diversity has become a competency that is instilled thoroughly through various curricular and co curricular activities. This has become quite apparent in the attitudes of the new generations and will enhance their contemplations. The movement for equality, which thought of long ago as the crux which hindered peace and justice has become very much an issue that continues to be improved within the country and in deed within diocesan boundaries. Once again as such a sensitive matter belongs very much to the conscience of each individual concerned, a general yes or no for equality cannot be expressed. Yet for such adjustment to take place in all aspects of faith administration the ideology of Christ like reconciliation needs to be sowed with intention.

Conclusion

The diocesan story is not at a conclusion but will continue to bring even greater insights into the concept of reconciliation. As the state of the nation and the mindset of the people who makes it up continues to be challenged globally and locally totally different reconciliations than what have been discussed may have to be dealt in future years. Yet we with all those who have gone before and the many to come pray the prayer that 'God of life , reconcile us', we remind ourselves of the many faces in which reconciliation has to be understood and has to be worked at drawing ever so closer to the truths that remain close to the heart of God.

Bibliography

1. (Ed) Anderson, Gerald.H., *The Theology of the Christian Mission* (London, Mcgraw-Hill Book Company, 1961).

2. (Ed) Karotemprel, Sebastian., *Following Christ in Mission* (India, Pauline Publication, 1995).

3. (Ed) Sharma, Arvind., *Women in World Religions* (Sri Satguru Publications, Delhi, 1995).

4. (Eds) England, John C., Kuttianimattathil, Jose., Mansford Prior, John., Quintos, Lily A., Kwang –sun, David Suh., Wickeri, Janice., *Asian Christian Theologies(Vol I)* (New York, Orbis Books, 2002).

5. (Eds) King, Sallie B., Queen, Christopher S., *Engaged Buddhism* (Albany, State University of New York Press, 1996).

6. Abeysingha, Nihal., *History of Christianity* (Colombo, Asian institute of Missiology, 2011)

7. Abeyasingha, Shanthi.,*The loud whisper theologizing in Sri Lanka today*– CSR 1980

8. Abayasekera, Jeffrey.,*The Christian Workers' Fellowship*

   Theological resources of the plantation workers

9. Balasunderam, Franklin J., *The Prophetic Voices of Asia (Part II)* (Sri Lanka, Centre for Society and Religion, 1994)

10. Balasuriya, Tissa., *Truth and the ambivalence of power*(Centre forSociety and Religion, Colombo 1997)

Truth and the ambivalence of power – Centre for Society and Religion Colombo 1997

*Buddhist Christian dialogue a controversy- CSR
Colombo 1990*

*Liberation trends in Hinduism Buddhism
Christianity and Islam _CSR Colombo 1987*

*Balasuriya, T. Vision for the future essays in honour of
TissaBalasuriya – CSR 1997*

*Balasuriya, Tissa Christian theology in Sri Lanka since
independence : 1948*

Jesus Christ and human liberation – CSR 1976

Right relationships CSR 1991

Jesus Kingdom church mission CSR 1990

Jesus Christ and human liberation CSR 1976

Planetary theology – Orbis books Maryknoll 1984

The development of the poor through the civilizing of the rich CSR 1972

11. Batumalai, S., *Asian Theology* (New Delhi, ISPCK, 1991).

12. Carter, J.R.F., *Religiousness in Sri Lanka* (Colombo, Marga Institute, 1979).

    Christianity and Islam _CSR Colombo 1987 Colombo 1990

13. Cosby, Jean., *How to Understand the History of Christian Mission* (London, SCM Press, 1966).

14. Dayal, Har., *The Bodhisattva Doctrine in Buddhist and Sankrit Literature* (Delhi, Motilal Banarsidass, 1932).

15. De Silva, L.A., *Why Cant I Save Myself* (Colombo, Dialogue Publications, 1966).

De Silva, Lynn A., *The Problem of the Self in Buddhism and Christianity* (Colombo, Study Centre for Religion and Society, 1975).

De Silva, Lynn., *Emergent Theology in the Context of Buddhism* (Colombo, Ecumenical Institute for Study and Dialogue, 1979).

De Silva, Lynn., *Logos, Vol 8, No. 2, The Buddhist Challenge and the Christian Response* (Colombo, Aquinas University College, 1967).

De Silva, Lynn A. Christian reflection in a Buddhist context

16. Devananda, Yohan. *Discovering new theology, new dharma, new ideology for post-tsunami*

17. England, John C., *Asian Christian Theologies*, Volume I (New York, Orbis Books, 2002).

18. Fernando, Keerthisiri*Religion as an agent of cultural and social change*

19. Furtado, Christopher L., *The Contribution of Dr. D.T Niles to the Church universal and Local* (Bangalore, United Theological College).

20. Gibbs, M. E., *From Jerusalem to New Delhi* (Madras, The Christian Literature Society, 1978, 145).

21. Gombrich, Richard., Obeyesekere, Gananath., *Buddhism Transformed* (New Jersey, Princeton University Press, 1988).

22. Huizinga, Johan., *Erasmus and the Age of Reformation* (New York, Harper Touchbooks , 1957).

23. Klostermaier, Klaus K., *A Short Introduction Buddhism* (Oxford, Oneworld Publications,

2006).

Liberation trends in Hinduism Buddhism

24. Niles D.T., *A decisive hour for the Christian Mission* (London, SCM Press, 1960).

25. Niles, D.T., *That they may have life* (New York, Harper & Brother Publishers, 1951).

26. Niles, D.T., *Upon the earth* (New York, Mcgraw –Hill Book company, 1962).

27. Peiris, Aloysius., *Love meets Wisdom* (New York, Orbis Books, 1988)

Prophetic humour in buddhis and Christianity –EISD Colombo 2005

Towards an Asian theology of liberation : some religio-cultural ..

God's reign for God's poor – Tulana Research Centre

Kalaniya 1999

An Ecumenically biblical approach to inter religious dialogue and inter – human justice

28. Perera, Leo., *Can they rise? a challenge to the laity today*

29. Perera, Somasiri., *Pastoral wisdom for inter-human justice – EISDColombo2011*

    Bishop Leo OSB an apostle for our time CSR 1963

    Bishop LEO the monk and prophet CSR 1993

30. Kulandran, Sabapathy*The word men and matters* _ The Institute forthe study of religion and society 1985

31. Rodrigo, Michael.,*Liberation : praxis*

32. Saddhatissa, H., *Buddhist Ethics* (London, George Allen & Unwin Ltd., 1970).

33. Sri Dhammanada, K., *What Buddhists Believe* (Taiwan, Corporate Body of the Buddha Educational Foundation, 1987).

34. Sri Dhammananda, K, *What Buddhists Believe* (Malaysia, Buddhist Missionary Society, 1987).

35. Wickremesinghe, Lakshman (Christianity in the context of other faiths)

Printed in Poland
by Amazon Fulfillment
Poland Sp. z o.o., Wrocław